Taverns in Town

A Pictorial Anthology
by
ALAN ROULSTONE

with Descriptive Text
by
MICHAEL ROULSTONE

FIRST EDITION 1973

BALFOUR PUBLICATIONS (PHOTO PRECISION LTD.)
ST. IVES, HUNTINGDON

IN ASSOCIATION WITH

TRAVELLERS REST PUBLICATIONS

ISBN 0 85944 001 X

Foreword

This selection of some of London's most popular and picturesque taverns is very deliberately termed an "anthology". A part of the reader's enjoyment, it is hoped, will be derived from finding omissions, personal favourites that are not represented. The compilers know this full well; at the same time they are confident that their selection will meet with many nods of satisfied approval.

Almost all the taverns are old ones; they fall basically into any of three distinct ages: that of Johnson, that of the Regency and that of Dickens; respectively, the second half of the eighteenth century, the early nineteenth century and the middle and later part of the nineteenth century. A few pre-date Johnson's day, a few are rather too late in date to have been known to Dickens.

It would thus have been an easy matter to compile a purely historical anthology; but the fact is that this would not have provided today's tavern frequenter with very much of practical interest. If he reads about an interesting establishment he requires it to be interesting still—that is, enjoyable. Therefore although most of these taverns are old they are also "contemporary", they carry out their contemporary duties in a commendable way. Here, in fact, is a selection of yesterday's taverns that are also very much the taverns of today.

The volume is arranged in a roughly geographical sequence. Without exception, food of greater or lesser ambitiousness is available in all the taverns, and in most cases during the evening as well as at lunchtime (though not always in such variety at night). Because of this, little mention is made in these pages of what kind of food is provided, but the reader will nevertheless discover that particular reference is made to facilities for eating wherever it seems appropriate (as where a separate restaurant exists, for example).

Contents

Chapter One

If the Thames as it passes through London fails wholly to characterise the capital city and does not, as do many other waterways, totally dominate the metropolis through which it flows, it is at any rate allowable to assert that without the presence of the Thames London could never have flowered. It is thus fitting to begin this brief survey of some of London's most popular taverns with one that lies Thames-side, in an area, moreover, that surely qualifies as being among the most picturesque spots in all of greater London. The tavern in question is THE KING'S ARMS, facing the Thames from a position of vantage on the Chelsea Embankment in Cheyne Walk (S.W.3.).

The situation of this fine old pub is for many of its patrons a primary advantage. Cheyne Walk and the area immediately surrounding it boast past associations with so many men and women of the world of art and literature that at any time when the weather is favourable it is safe to assume that pilgrims of one worthy or another will be in the neighbourhood, and a good many of them will call in at the King's Head in passing. Presumably it is Thomas Carlyle, the great historian and man of culture whose house in nearby Cheyne Row has been turned into a museum, that most of these visitors are pursuing; but many other people also lived here. The painter Turner and another painter, Daniel Maclise, the novelist George Eliot and the painter and poet Dante Gabriel Rossetti all lived in Cheyne Walk itself at different times; while in a house that actually stands alongside the King's Arms lived a famous painter of a more recent era, Philip Wilson Steer. It is fitting that such an excellent tavern as this should be at hand to answer the requirements of the inquisitive today.

The King's Arms lies only a few yards away from the river and close to the famous Botanic Gardens just off the Chelsea Embankment. Also of great interest is its close proximity to Crosby Hall, the ancient residence of Sir John Crosby and now standing on a site once occupied by the gardens of Sir Thomas More's residence. The building dates from 1466, having been physically removed from its original position in Bishopsgate. At one time it came into the hands of Sir Thomas More, long before its removal to Chelsea, and it is thus fitting that the persons responsible for its removal should have selected the present tract of ground.

The King's Arms' own history boasts nothing of such extreme interest as this; however, it dates back at least to 1785, and conceivably even earlier. Cheyne Walk did not then exist, at any rate not in name. A brew house stood beside the King's Arms in the eighteenth century and presumably, as was then the general custom, it served the tavern itself, for most landlords brewed their own beer. Later the property was rented to independent brewers. During this same early period it would appear that the King's Arms was also a residential inn, though it is so no longer; and this indeed is true of virtually every old inn of London. At the same time also it boasted extensive grounds that reached right down to the banks of the Thames, and happily it is still not too difficult to picture this now vanished prospect.

Today this is an extremely busy Chelsea tavern, its antiquity immediately attested by its old flagstone floors. The river frontage continues to bestow upon it a certain distinction, of the kind that makes the Londoner at any rate glad that he is a Londoner, and glad that such pleasing places of distraction are dotted about the city to gratify his more expansive and congenial instincts.

There are of course many of them. Chelsea abounds with them; but at the same time it needs to be said that there are several pubs in the area, at one time eminently worthy of patronage, that today either exist no more or else function as discothèques or worse. These last perhaps possess their own attractions, but they find no place in a selection such as this. It is therefore heartening to be able still to record so many very good Chelsea taverns, and if some are missing here it is only for lack of space.

The King's Arms —
CHEYNE WALK

THE PHOENIX in Smith Street (S.W.3.) is just such a pub, lying only a step away from the busy King's Road, a few minutes walk from Sloane Square. It stands at the heart of a part of Chelsea steeped in historical associations: south of the King's Road and in an area that extends down to the river. It is here, between Smith Street and the Thames, that the Royal Hospital stands, founded by King Charles II and designed by Sir Christopher Wren. This is of course the home of the colourfully attired Chelsea Pensioners, several of whom are regular patrons at the Phoenix.

Alongside the grounds of the Royal Hospital, running down to the embankment at Chelsea Bridge, stand Ranelagh Gardens, originally conceived as eighteenth century Chelsea's answer to Vauxhall Gardens on the other, the allegedly unfashionable side of the water. With its famous rotunda, where patrons used to describe graceful circumnavigations, taking occasional refreshment, now and then pausing to take heed of the band and the popular vocalists of the day, Ranelagh attempted a little more in the way of respectability than was thought necessary at Vauxhall. There were however blemishes: the gardens, in their more unillumined reaches, just as at the transpontine resort, provided pickpockets and ladies of the town with all the shroud of darkness they desired.

Gentlemen however wore swords, and it is always possible that they relished a chance encounter with a pickpocket as an opportunity to practise their swordsmanship. Even Dr. Johnson, who did not wear a sword, felt no qualms at raising his stick one evening and threatening to drub an unfortunate pyrotechnician who had resolved not to set off his fireworks because it was too damp. The doctor threatened a riot, and the man was forced to begin with his display; but he had been right all along, and they failed to do anything other than fizzle.

Outwardly an air of steadfast decorum used to be preserved at Ranelagh, and it permeated the entire neighbourhood. It is still in evidence: such polite functions as the annual Chelsea Flower Show, or many spacious and gracefully laid out thoroughfares lined by fine town mansions that have defied the trend towards transmogrification into apartment buildings, all characterise a part of London into which such a tavern as the Phoenix, with its good array of hot and cold bar food and its air of being a little removed from bustle, fits most successfully and naturally.

On a summer's afternoon over the weekend, when the surrounding streets are relatively tranquil and tables and chairs are set out on the pavement beside the Phoenix, it is a thoroughly relaxing place to take a drink. It is difficult to keep in mind that the garish and noisy King's Road is so close to hand, not at all difficult to recall that Chelsea, when it was no more than a village, used, on account of the large number of wealthy people who established riverside residences just to the south of where the Phoenix now stands, to be called the "Village of Palaces".

The Phoenix . . .
SMITH STREET

On the opposite, the north side of the King's Road, there are other reminders of this fact. For where there were gentry there were villagers as well, and facing what was at one time the Chelsea village green there is another excellent tavern, THE RED HOUSE, Elystan Street (S.W.3.), reached from the King's Road by way of Markham Street. The interior is much altered from its original state, for it has to cater to a very heavy lunchtime custom and for this purpose provides extensive and substantial snack food; outside it still presents something of the appearance of a village pub, even though the green has long since vanished.

This is a tavern well worth taking note of, perhaps for when one visits nearby Chelsea Town Hall, setting for so many concerts and other functions, including the annual Antiques Fair, and wishes to escape as quickly as possible from the King's Road. It lies amid houses that by and large are smaller than those to be discovered on the south side of the King's Road; but this is a fashionable residential district nevertheless, and the Red House enjoys a steady local trade.

The Red House
ELYSTAN STREET

It lies within two or three minutes walk of another excellent Chelsea tavern to the north of the King's Road, one built at approximately the same time. But whereas THE BUILDERS ARMS in Britten Street (S.W.3.) was erected especially to serve the needs of the masons and other workmen employed in building St. Luke's Church just opposite, erected during 1820–1824, The Red House was established to cater to the parishioners. The builders in question, in putting up a church in the style of the then popular Gothic revival, incidentally graced St. Luke's with the first stone groined roof to be placed on an English church since the days of the Reformation.

It is an interesting circumstance that the first rector appointed to the living of St. Luke's was the Hon. Gerald Wellesley, brother to the "Iron" Duke of Wellington. But of even greater interest is the fact that it was in this church, in 1836, that the man who knew and loved London (and her taverns) perhaps better than any man of the nineteenth century was married. This was, of course, Charles Dickens. He mentioned neither the Red House nor the Builders Arms in his writings, but he would surely have

at least observed the latter, and it is not beyond feasibility to suggest that he may have patronised it.

No longer the domain of carpenters and stone masons, the Builders Arms is highly popular among nearby residents, who frequent it in large numbers. The interior is spacious and pleasingly decorated with wrought-iron work. The array of food available at the bar is really extensive, and constitutes one of the Builders Arms' principal features.

Both it and the Red House are fortunate in

that they are situated in what is virtually a little backwater of Chelsea, literally within a minute's walk of the King's Road and yet wholly removed from its more unpleasant and unwholesome manifestations. Both of them, from their exterior appearances at least, seem as though they have overcome the imposition of trends now favoured by the more impudent of Chelsea-ites. The small patch of greenery allowed by St. Luke's Church, like the little clump of trees which is all that remains of the original village green in front of the Red House, helps to give the Builders Arms something of the character of a village inn.

At some little distance from these two houses, in Eaton Terrace (S.W.1.), stands the well known and extremely popular DUKE OF WELLINGTON, named after the rector of St. Lukes' brother. One of the most attractive and comfortable of all Chelsea taverns, the Duke of Wellington has stood on the same spot for over 250 years now; though a moment's reflection will easily uncover the elementary fact that it has not always borne the name it now boasts, nor the same excellent sign, a three-quarter length portrait of the Duke painted by Vere Temple and affixed to the side of the house in 1935.

Following his victory at Waterloo and his subsequent popularity as a parliamentarian, Arthur Wellesley, Duke of Wellington, became accountable for changes in pub names almost beyond count. It has often been pointed out how many a name of perhaps historical significance has vanished beyond recall by the simple act of a fervid landlord of a past age making a gesture of patriotism in an eager determination to draw equally fervid patrons to his own establishment. What name this Duke of Wellington previously bore is unknown.

Situated where Belgravia merges with Chelsea, between Eaton Square and Sloane Square in one of fashionable London's most permanently popular areas, the Duke of Wellington lies sufficiently far removed from the main thoroughfares to escape the patronage of the merely boisterous. Despite this, and in part because of it, the tavern is busy virtually always.

Chelsea has always enjoyed a reputation for being the territory of bohemia, a centre of artistic activity. True or not, it has always been obvious to even the most cursory observer that people with proper artistic pretensions have kept themselves just slightly aloof from the bizarre and sometimes hollow artiness of public Chelsea. The Duke of Wellington, on the very perimeter of this miniature city within a city, can stare incredulously in at the less staid carryings-on of some of Chelsea's more exotic inhabitants.

The Duke of Wellington is convenient for patrons of the Royal Court Theatre in Sloane Square. It may claim the privilege of catering to a by and large refined clientele; it also provides an excellent hot and cold buffet counter which attracts not only business people for their lunchtime bite to eat but local residents for a plate of hot food that constitutes a complete evening meal. Also in Eaton Terrace, though a couple of minutes walk away from the Duke of Wellington, just at the back of Sloane Square itself, there is another equally good pub, one moreover that in the past used to thrive on its reputation for being the haunt of those citizens of bohemia who lived hereabouts. The pub in question is of course THE ANTELOPE, certainly one of the best known taverns in this part of London.

The good thing about the Antelope is that it does not seem to change very much. Here a gentle unpretentiousness mingles easily with a pleasing touch of refinement, even dignity; while there is just sufficient of informality to allow the abandonment of inhibitions for a short while, which is surely the true function of the English inn or tavern. People call in at the Antelope year after year, some with regularity, some only as their other enterprises allow, and they know they will always find just the same pub they ever knew. The old wood-panelled walls remain as always; so too does the excellent restaurant, highly praised for its simple, good food cooked in a traditional English manner.

The name of this celebrated Chelsea tavern derives from the coat of arms of King Henry V, but there the connection ends: the Antelope is not that old. It lies conveniently placed for Sloane Street and Sloane Square shoppers, a welcome little retreat in what year by year becomes an increasingly hectic portion of the metropolis. It possesses, however, one other most important characteristic: for if this part of London boasts a true "local"

Duke of Wellington ...
EATON TERRACE

The Antelope . . .
EATON TERRACE

then the Antelope may lay claim to being it. Chelsea Pensioners use this tavern regularly, so do military personnel from the nearby barracks just off the King's Road; but this is a democratic institution, and there are many others. Most of the surrounding residences are the homes of fairly well-to-do people, and many of them frequent this pub a good deal; so does a host of domestic employees of one kind or another who serve the blocks of flats and other properties in the neighbourhood. This facet is of course most prominent during the evening; at lunchtime, like virtually every other tavern described in these pages, the Antelope caters to a surge of invaders from offices and other places of business. Thus it is that this tavern is probably best savoured later on at night, between nine and ten perhaps, before theatregoers begin to quench the thirsts they have been nurturing throughout an evening's performance at the Royal Court Theatre. At such an hour it really is possible here to imbibe a little of late nineteenth century atmosphere; and if there are no longer painterly aspirants sitting long over "small beers", smoking decrepid pipes osten-tatiously and dreaming of fame, then at any rate there remains that elusive property loosely defined as "character".

The foregoing taverns make up just a small selection of some of those worth sampling in the one-time village of Chelsea. Leaving Chelsea and travelling slightly northwards one arrives at that other popular hive of bohemia, South Kensington. It is an area one still associates with art students, infesters of the museums that proliferate hereabouts, exiles from improbable eastern European countries who inhabit diminutive bed-sitters crammed with books and mementoes of past existences, together with a host of other miscellaneous intellectuals and semi-intellectuals. And even if this is no longer a completely accurate picture of the inhabitants of this part of London, there still hangs about South Kensington a hazily defined atmosphere of refinement placed through no fault of its own in reduced circumstances.

Two taverns may be singled out within the immediate vicinity of South Kensington underground station. The first is THE HOUR GLASS in

The Hour Glass ..
BROMPTON ROAD .

Brompton Road (S.W.3.). It is needless to explain why this tavern should be known locally as the "Wedge". It precisely resembles one. Moreover, it is one of the pubs, two or three of which crop up in these pages, with a claim to be among the smallest in London. Lack of space is thus a distinct feature; but it does not prevent the establishment from providing full-scale hot luncheons and an array of other bar food, nor does it tempt patrons to stay away on account of possible discomfort. They come in large numbers.

One of the Hour Glass' most pleasing features springs directly from its location. Just around the corner from the pub is an open-air fruit and vegetable market, and the street is lined with small shops of one kind or another, conducted by a deeply entrenched body of ordinary London trades-people. As a reminder however of the multifariousness of London's populace, also around the corner from the Hour Glass, in another direction, lies a highly fashionable residential sector, centred about Egerton Gardens. It was in adjoining Egerton Place, only a minute's walk from the Hour Glass, that the popular nineteenth century dramatist and journalist, Douglas Jerrold, lived; and it was here

17

that he first met Charles Dickens. Alas, this is another tavern that the great novelist could have known but made no mention of in his writings.

The interior of this good little public house has been pleasingly fitted out to present all the comforts contemporary patrons demand. Little hint of the nineteenth century is provided here today, but perhaps its diversity of patronage, occasioned by its situation, allows just a glimpse of the tavern life of a past age. A painting hanging on one of the walls entitled "The Last Stage on the Portsmouth Road" aptly hints at the Hour Glass' respectably antique origins, as well as to its one-time calling.

The Hour Glass stands at the point where Brompton Road and Fulham Road merge. Old Brompton Road (S.W.7.), which runs more or less parallel to the latter for a short way, lies just slightly to the north. It is the area about this road, and the neighbourhood lying between it and the Cromwell Road, that over the decades has come to symbolise for many the kind of area where artists, scholars and other people of like temperament delight to congregate. The Royal College of Art is only a few hundred yards away, and many famous artists have lived hereabouts over the years; indeed, early in the twentieth century a loosely associated group of painters was generally referred to as the "Cromwell Road School".

Bearing this in mind, it is not surprising that at the head of Old Brompton Road, a minute's walk from Cromwell Road, also from the South Kensington underground station, there stands a public house that in many ways epitomises what the busy London tavern is at its best. This is THE ZETLAND. Its success and popularity stem from several factors, and it is of interest to take them in order, for they demonstrate characteristics that are true of almost all the taverns mentioned in these pages.

Most regular tavern users in London will count high among their list of priorities the provision of good food: in this department the Zetland can certainly equal any other, and surpass a good many, for it has an excellent buffet counter, and anything from a sandwich to a full-scale hot lunch is to be procured here. Another important feature, for many, is the availability of a reasonable amount of comfortable seating; and here again the Zetland can claim more than sympathetic attention. Last but not least of course must be the range of spirits and liqueurs behind the bar and in this too the Zetland is exceptionally well equipped. Thus on every count this South Kensington tavern that enjoys a considerable patronage is worthy of a visit. But even with all these features, without a varied clientele and without a distinct personality of its own no public house can be anything other than a purely functional institution, meting out drinks to lunchtime business people and those who have a few minutes to spare in the evening after work before hurrying off to the station to catch the train home. Happily the Zetland has succeeded in avoiding such a character.

It draws its custom, especially at lunchtime, from a vast cross-section of local working people, from shop assistants to employees of the numerous museums nearby; it also boasts a strong local contingent, in evidence especially during the evening. This is essentially an active pub; and for the stranger who wishes to sample at first hand a little typical London life as manifested in the bonhomie of the pub, this is the place to come to. In addition, it exists as a most forceful reminder of what is the difference between a country pub and a London tavern: its patrons do not visit it,

The Zetland – BROMPTON ROAD

they use it, it is a positive part of their lives. People come to a pub such as this to while away an entire evening in conversation; but for some reason they do not as a result cause it to seem a private club.

Both the Zetland and the Hour Glass lie on the fringe of what used to be the isolated village of Brompton, where during the eighteenth century people used to journey in vain attempts to banish consumption, on account of Brompton being on a lower level than other parts of London and thus—at least in theory—a little warmer. Then Brompton was separated from the city of Westminster by what was virtually open countryside, through which it was dangerous to pass at night for fear of attack by footpads or gangs of young "bloods" bent upon enjoying themselves in riot and folly. Between what is today Hyde Park Corner, where St. George's Hospital stands, and Brompton there stood Kensington Palace, set amid lovely gardens that are today a public park. It was here, in 1819, that Queen Victoria was born.

Today Kensington Palace is partly given over to the London Museum, but during the nineteenth century and earlier it was an important royal residence, and it was to house ladies of the court, about 1860, that Beauchamp Place (S.W.3.), just off Brompton Road, was laid out. It is in this colourful little street that THE GROVE TAVERN is to be discovered.

Beauchamp Place is one of the most consistently pleasing thoroughfares in London, both for its appearance and for the kind of goods offered for sale in the small shops that line it on either side. It has often been remarked that although there is a unity to the architecture displayed by the shops in this street, there is such a variety of commerce being pursued that a permanent and invigorating disparity is achieved. It is a satisfying street to stroll along, and by good fortune the Grove Tavern not only fits into it by virtue of its appearance but also for its general excellence.

Before Beauchamp Place was established, the land where it now stands was occupied by market gardens. Until 1885 it was actually known under the more appropriate name of Grove Place, and of course it is from this that the Grove Tavern derives its name. It was at about this date, or possibly just slightly before, that the Grove Tavern was first opened, during the same period indeed when nearby Brompton Oratory was being built, which dates from 1884—though there is not said to be any connection between the two establishments! Before the Grove became a public house the present property consisted of two separate residences, which, like all the others in the street, housed ladies in waiting.

The 1880's mark the time when Brompton ceased to be a partially out-lying suburb of greater London and succumbed to total annexation, so that before long it seemed it was no more than a sector of South Kensington. The process of integration has continued until today hardly any vestige of the old village remains, although some of the residential streets lying at the back of Beauchamp Place cling to a semblance of quietude that is not very typical of London, and Brompton Square, two or three minutes walk away from the Grove Tavern, still presents a decided air of peacefulness. For long this latter provided merchants, successful actors and other worthies whose presence was required daily in the City or in Westminster with places of refuge from the rush of their professional activities, and numerous well known people lived here during the eighteenth and nineteenth centuries.

The Grove Tavern ...
BEAUCHAMP PLACE

For the visitor who wishes to explore this part of London the Grove is an ideal place to pause at for refreshment. It boasts a good array of snack food, to be eaten if one so wishes off now quite rare marble-topped tables. It is a small pub, exuding an air of well-being, while upstairs it possesses a first class restaurant with a good menu and a fine selection of table wines.

The Grove lies only a little distance away from what is one of London's most fashionable shopping centres. It is at times heartening to recall, perhaps during a sudden shower of rain when taxis become unprocurable, that most of this was open countryside less than two centuries ago, not crowded with shoppers some of whom seem to have no idea at all where they are going or what they wish to buy. With a little sprightly walking it is in any case possible to leave them far behind, and make off in the direction of Hyde Park Corner. A little before this landmark, on the right hand side of the road, almost hidden from view, is a narrow alleyway that bears the name of Old Barrack Yard. Passing along here, into a veritable maze of smartly apportioned mews, one comes upon one of the most celebrated taverns in town.

This is THE GRENADIER in Wilton Row (S.W.I.). The barracks that at one time stood nearby were those to which the Duke of Wellington was once attached, and it is said that he and his officers used to patronise the Grenadier regularly. Their horses were stabled in the mews just at the back of the pub; and some will claim that the steps leading up to the front door were at one time a mounting block and that the "Iron" Duke himself used frequently to employ them. Today, apart from the portrait of a Grenadier that provides a signboard for this famous tavern, there is an old guard-box standing outside as a reminder of its past military associations.

Inside there are numerous other reminders. Military prints and other curios adorn the walls, and even the bartenders are habited to resemble army mess stewards; and more significant than all these things, the Grenadier is still a regular haunt of army officers. With its pewter-topped bar

The Grenadier
WILTON ROW

counter, its excellent buffet bar and small restaurant, its low-ceilinged back room, it is of course peopled by an entire cross-section of society, and is in no way an exclusively military establishment.

It lies at the end of a private cobbled road on the Grosvenor estate where even now a gate is still lowered at a certain hour each night. However, bucks no longer topple over the guard in his box as they would have done in the age of the Regency when that pastime was considered one of the more amusing distractions to be essayed during an evening out, and when unfortunate watchmen, once overturned, had to remain in their horizontally imprisoned positions until more kindly passers-by righted them. Then, as now, the bucks were frequently young army officers, and like their counterparts today, they would have known the Grenadier.

It is always a pleasing fact to contemplate, in a London depleted of so many of its older features, that in Grosvenor Mews, one of the approaches to the Grenadier, by way of Grosvenor Crescent, horses are still stabled. Almost exclusively, London mews properties today have become private residences, or else garages, and it is somehow fitting that in a neighbourhood once given over so fully as this one was to the stabling of military horses, near to a tavern that still seems to echo to the chatter of Wellington and his youthful cronies, there should be this very firm reminder of what a mews properly existed for.

One pleasing feature of the narrow mews crowded together here is that they are all closed to ordinary traffic. As a result, only taxis and residents' own vehicles may drive up to the Grenadier. Thus it is that in the summer, when the vine that flowers outside this tavern has assumed its wonted extravagance and when drinkers like to take their glasses outside to lounge about the steps or upon benches, there are no bothersome motor engines to interrupt their tranquility and discourse. Traffic thunders along Knightsbridge a hundred yards away, and it is of no consequence at all to customers at the Grenadier.

Wilton Row may also be gained by way of Wilton Crescent. A little further along from its place of access, off Wilton Place, lies a narrow thoroughfare known as Kinnerton Street (S.W.1.), whose southern end gives off into Motcomb Street, itself now graced by the presence of Sotheby's Belgravia auction rooms. There are four pubs in Kinnerton Street, and the two selected here present a fine contrast to one another. The first, THE NAG'S HEAD, is celebrated for being the smallest tavern in town. In fact the claim is debatable, but it is certainly among the smallest and it is in every way a "gem".

A primary attraction lies in its steadfast refusal to bow before the tyrant progress; indeed, Kinnerton Street itself, despite the unbecoming modernity that has invaded the patch of it facing the second recommended pub to be discovered there, the Turk's Head, retains a partly nineteenth century flavour. The Nag's Head, with its deep-stained walls, its slightly neglected appearance that at once endears it to the hardened pub enthusiast, its old china beer handles that once secured a prize at a brewers' exhibition, and

The Nags Head~~
KINNERTON STREET

most of all its total unpretentiousness, easily convey one back a century in time, to an era when, as the name of this tavern indicates, horses and their grooms were busy just outside.

This part of Kinnerton Street abounds in little courts and small houses, and the Nag's Head fits naturally into its setting. It is of course a local, but its popularity extends wider than one might imagine, for it is one of the taverns that Americans and other visitors from overseas will most likely have read about in advance of visiting London, and they flock to it. Local business people also come here; and of course the seasoned London pub crawler inevitably includes it high on his list. What it is that attracts people to a little pub such as this is hard to define: perhaps the answer lies in the very basic human desire to forsake plushness from time to time and resort to somewhere that is down-to-earth. This the Nag's Head certainly is, and because it is it succeeds in seeming precisely what one always imagines a hidden-away little mews pub of yesteryear ought to be like but alas so seldom is.

Simple snack food is provided at the Nag's Head, but not in any great variety. There is not the available space, either for serving or for consuming. Having paused a while at this worthwhile little pub, therefore, the stranger would be well advised to wander along Kinnerton Street to the other end and call in at THE TURK'S HEAD. Stepping inside, he will at once detect something unusual about the feeling of the place, but probably it will require several minutes for him to hit upon what it is that causes this strangeness: for the illumination at the Turk's Head, with the exception of concealed lighting behind the bar, is provided by old fashioned gas lamps. This is not unique in a London tavern, but it is certainly rare, and bestows a most pleasing atmosphere upon the long room that constitutes the single bar of this popular establishment.

A plaque outside the main entrance of the Turk's Head claims that this early Victorian structure was originally the site of the Turk's Head Coffee House, in which in 1764 Dr. Johnson, Reynolds the painter, Boswell, Burke and others founded the Literary Society. Unfortunately, this simply is not the case; and anybody acquainted with Dr. Johnson's habits must know that

The Turks Head _ _ _
KINNERTON STREET

he would never have strayed so far away from his beloved Fleet Street and its environs. The Turk's Head Coffee House with Johnsonian associations was the one that lay in the Strand.

It is however forgivable for this tavern to claim such an association, for its own literary connections, in the later age of Dickens and Thackeray, are numerous. Prints about its walls of nineteenth century literary worthies highlight this fact. More interestingly, at the far end of the bar, on open shelves, there is a small collection of leather-bound books, and among them are some original volumes of Dickens' periodical called "All the Year Round".

One would speak in terms of the "setting", rather than the "decor", of the Turk's Head, but whatever the term employed it is graceful and extremely comfortable, with thick carpeting and a row of leather covered seats laid out so as to present virtually a series of divided compartments. There is plenty of counter room to order drinks or to stand and talk, and at one end of the bar there is a buffet counter. Upstairs there is also a restaurant.

The exterior too is of considerable interest. There are not all that many taverns of the same name in London; there are certainly no others adorned about their facades by little busts of Turks with turbans, as plaques beneath each head indicate, formed from the colours of famous Rugby football clubs. The Ironsides R.F.C., the Old Belvedere R.F.C. and the London Irish R.F.C. are among the names thus uniquely represented. In every way this is surely an unusual pub; it is gratifying therefore to find that it is also an extremely good one, lying as it does on the fringe of Belgravia, only one minute's walk away from polite Belgrave Square which was laid out in 1845, at about the same date as this tavern was erected, and which W. S. Gilbert, the "Bab Balladist", thought the most aristocratic square in all London.

The Windsor Castle . . .
CAMPDEN HILL ROAD

Returning further west, this time to the north of Kensington Gardens, on Campden Hill Road (W.8.), which runs between Notting Hill Gate and Kensington High Street, there is another tavern worthy of mention in these pages, and that is THE WINDSOR CASTLE, a house that from the outside almost resembles a country pub set down in the middle of a city.

The location of this excellent establishment is of particular interest, for to its south lie gracious residences, and many a hint of even grander houses of the past. Campden Hill and Campden Hill Road are today the only reminders of Campden House which once stood nearby, while the entire area is one with a glittering array of one-time literary, artistic and fashionable associations. The Holland House Circle, a loosely defined cross-section of wits, noblemen and men of culture of the early nineteenth century who came together under the auspices of the third Lord Holland at his home close by, still seems to exert an influence over this very pleasant neighbourhood, and many indeed are those who visit these parts every year. Byron, Wilberforce, Talleyrand, Macaulay are just a few of the earlier names that spring to mind. Macaulay himself actually lived on Campden Hill, at Holly Lodge, next door to the Duke of Argyll. Both men were jealous of the quiet they were able to secure in the neighbourhood, and in many ways it has lingered. The Windsor Castle fits admirably into this setting, and the curious visitor will no doubt remember it.

The oak panelling in the bars, installed during the 1930's, together with the copper, pewter and ceramic curios that decorate them, lend this tavern an atmosphere of antique comfort. Good hot and cold bar food consolidates the house's other amenities, while an attractive sherry bar adds to the pleasure of dropping in here. A garden provides summer drinkers with the opportunity to take their glasses out of doors, and in a part of London that has always been proud of its pastoral recesses, both large and small, this is somehow more than fitting.

Travelling east, Notting Hill Gate merges with the Bayswater Road (W.2.), and as anybody who has journeyed along here well knows, facing Kensington Gardens almost opposite Lancaster Walk, the wide footpath running across the gardens down to the Albert Memorial, there stands a fine tavern by the name of THE SWAN.

This pub lies about half way along Bayswater Road. At the eastern end of the road today stands Marble Arch, originally designed to stand in front of Buckingham Palace but reputedly found to be too narrow to allow the passage of the royal coach and later placed here as a compromise. Tyburn Tree, London's notorious gallows, upon which numerous well known characters paid the ultimate penalty, stood here until 1783. It was in 1760 that the infamous Claude Duval, subject of a variety of fictional creations over the years, met the usual fate accorded to convicted highwaymen. It is said that when his body was put on public display afterwards it was avidly inspected by crowds of fashionable people, mostly of the female sex. Tyburn was a fitting place for the Frenchman's execution: for this one-time page at the court of King Charles II frequently "worked" what is today the Bayswater Road.

The Swan did not of course exist in Duval's day. Instead, on the site which it now occupies there stood, at least during the latter part of the eighteenth century, the popular Bayswater, or Floral Tea Gardens, of which the Swan is very properly a reminder. Here Londoners would come for purposes of recreation in much the same way that today they might be likely to go out for the day to Brighton. It was still possible in those days to enjoy real country air in the vicinity; and even now, because the Swan stands a little way back off the main road, facing Kensington Gardens and providing summer imbibers with tables and chairs set outside upon what almost amounts to a terrace, an air of festive informality lingers.

Probably the Swan dates from about the year 1800, though no actual records are in existence for the period prior to 1829. It nestles perfectly at ease beneath the imposing blocks of Lancaster Gate, erected during the middle of the nineteenth century and themselves standing on the site of the old Victoria Tea Gardens, oblivious to the constant drumming of traffic passing by. It is generously spacious within, with restaurant facilities as well as a magnificent display of bar food that invariably includes a whole turkey and several other large cuts of meat.

The Swan lies a minute's walk away from Lancaster Gate underground station, and as it invariably happens that good pubs come not singly but in clusters it is not surprising to find that in the area immediately surrounding this station there are at least two other very worthwhile taverns. THE ARCHERY TAVERN in Bathurst Street (W.2.) is a most pleasing establishment. From the outside it appears no more than an ordinary, unpretentious tavern, with a small but neat frontage; within it is surprisingly spacious, with wooden partitions separating the different portions of the bar.

The Archery dates back to the reign of King George II, and therefore pre-dates the Swan quite considerably, but the interior decor now in evidence is no more than a century old. Long since converted for other purposes are the original yard and stables, and of course the open land that once characterised this area is no more. The Archery is surrounded on all sides by housing blocks, intersected by a sometimes bewildering maze of fairly uniform streets where it is the easiest thing in the world, if one is unused to them, to become lost. Even so, there is an authentic touch of yesteryear about this recommended tavern, and it is a most popular and delightful little place.

The name is somewhat unusual. It stems from the year 1821 when the members of the Toxophilite Society had a pavilion on this site where they practised their difficult art until 1834, after which they removed to Regent's Park. Even more interesting is the nearby presence of Westbourne Street, a matter only of some twenty yards from the front door of the Archery Tavern. This roadway denotes the passage of the "lost" (that is underground) Westbourne River, that used to flow openly from Hampstead Heath down to the Thames near what is now Chelsea Bridge and naturally provided one of the major assets of the nearby Bayswater Tea Gardens.

When the Westbourne flowed openly it was known at this stretch of its journey Thames-ward as Baynard's Water, from which is derived the name Bayswater. It journeyed south from here along a course marking what is today the division between Hyde Park and Kensington Gardens, two or three minutes walk away from the Archery Tavern. Here the Westbourne is still to be observed: for the Serpentine, one of London's best loved patches of water, is in fact a short stretch of it, widened to fulfil its present function.

The Swan
BAYSWATER ROAD

WATKEYS

C

The Archery Tavern . . .
BATHURST STREET

How many Londoners are aware of this? Very few, to be sure, and it is always interesting to contemplate such past phenomena. If a particular tavern may be conjoined with one's reflections, all to the good; and where better than the Archery Tavern? There is however just one more tavern in this area where the enthusiast might like to call. This is to be found in nearby Strathearn Place (W.2.) and is called THE VICTORIA TAVERN. Not so old as the Archery, as its name for one thing reveals, the Victoria is nevertheless a fine nineteenth century tavern, fitted out quite luxuriously and extremely popular with local residents. Both the Victoria and the Archery lie in a small segment of territory, falling between the intersection of the Bayswater Road and Edgware Road, that, for obvious reasons, is sometimes known as Tyburnia; though the macabre associations of that name can in no way be connected with the rows of large and elegant mansions that were mainly erected during the 1840's.

The Victoria fits agreeably into this setting, for it is a tall, typically high-Victorian structure, adorned within by all the appurtenances of solid comfort. It became nationally famous a few years ago when a painting hanging on its walls was discovered after restoration to be a valuable portrait of a past member of the royal family; as a most laudable gesture it was presented as a gift to the Queen and added to the royal portrait collection.

This is but one agreeable thing about the Victoria; another is the collection of theatrical memorabilia housed in the upstairs "Gaiety Room", or perhaps the restaurant known as "Our Mutual Friend"; but most of all it is its immediately discernible atmosphere of being a highly favoured public house that gives this tavern its main appeal. No evidence can be adduced for the Victoria having been at any time connected with the nearby Victoria Tea Gardens already referred to; but at any rate it is worth mentioning that the name of this recommended tavern need not necessarily have been derived directly from that of the monarch then occupying the throne.

The Victoria ~~~
STRATHEARN PLACE

Chapter Two

To the Londoner, one of the capital city's most attractive features is its profusion of outlying areas, at one time quite independent communities but now a part of the mass of greater London, that yet still cling to something of their isolated past and provide him with little niches of territory where he may repair for strictly restorative purposes. Such areas include Chiswick and Putney to the south, Hampstead and Highgate to the north. Before turning to these two latter and singling out a few of their finer public houses —in itself no hardship, for they are many—one other area, St. John's Wood, just to the north west of Regent's Park, may also be glanced at, and no problem is presented when one is required to place a finger not only on one of the best taverns in that area but indeed in the whole of greater London. For here is to be found THE STAR, on the corner of St. John's Wood Terrace and Charlbert Street (N.W.8.).

As the name suggests, during the seventeenth century there was thick woodland in this part of London, providing a favourite hiding place for highwaymen and other malefactors who wished to elude their lawful pursuers. Even at the beginning of the nineteenth century St. John's Wood could still boast much open countryside; but today it is a thickly populated residential area, with many of the one-time rows of terrace houses having disappeared of late to make way for large apartment blocks. How fortunate therefore that there remains this little village pub: for that is what the Star in truth is, a local of distinction, resorted to by nearby residents and visitors from other parts of London alike.

Once the property of the powerful Knights Hospitallers, this part of London was during its heyday in the nineteenth century the home of many artists. Copley the painter is buried in St. John's Wood churchyard, a minute or two's walk away from the Star; Landseer lived in St. John's Wood Road; and there were many others. They bestowed upon the area something of an air of refinement, and happily it has been passed down over the years. Into this setting the Star fits admirably.

There is of course another attraction, and that is the proximity of the famous Lord's cricket ground, Mecca of enthusiasts from all over the world, not a few of whom wend their way towards the Star. This was not Lord's first ground in London; that was established in what is now Dorset Square, just off Baker Street, in 1782, but the present ground has been operational ever since about 1810. The Star would itself have been in existence by that time: it boasts some fine old beams and a most genuine antique flavour.

The Star Inn.
ST. JOHNS WOOD

Copper and brass decorate the walls, and there is an interesting collection of model galleons about the bar. Here, indeed, is a really worthwhile public house.

Further north, up in Highgate Village (N.6.), is yet another celebrated old tavern, one of many to be discovered in this village on a hill from which at one time it was possible—though it is so no longer—to obtain a prospect of the entire metropolis, then separated from Highgate by a respectable expanse of open countryside. The tavern chosen for inclusion here is THE FLASK, the present building of which dates from 1767, though the inn itself is a good deal older.

During the eighteenth century there used to be a number of Highgate inns at which the stage coaches into and out of London called. In these houses, of which the Flask was one, a curious ceremony known as "swearing on the horn" was observed; and indeed this was one of the village's principal claims to fame, together with the comparatively healthy atmosphere to be enjoyed there. The ceremony consisted basically of causing uninitiated strangers from passing coaches to buy wine, and required them to kiss a pair of bullock's horns mounted on a five foot pole before which the ceremony of initiation was performed. Fortunately for the unwitting stranger, in its later forms the ceremony gave a choice between kissing either the pair of horns or a pretty girl if there happened to be one present. It is said that the custom may have sprung from the time when Highgate was an important overnight resting place for drovers, and that landlords introduced this gimmick as a means of securing their custom. However, the true origins of this practice are lost in antiquity and it is possible that they embody an element of religious significance.

The Flask can point to numerous past associations of fame and notoriety. William Hogarth the painter is certainly to be counted among the most illustrious, and it is said to have been at the Flask that one of his companions once hit a villager on the head with a pint pot and caused such a flow of blood that the amused artist was prompted to make an on-the-spot sketch of the unfortunate man. Dick Turpin is also thought to have come here, to hide in the cellars. Whether or not this claim can be substantiated is open to debate: the redoubtable highwayman is supposed to have frequented so many taverns.

The Flask

HIGHGATE

Rowlestone 73

Today the Flask is an attractive village pub on the outskirts of north London, extremely popular and rarely uncrowded. Its facade is beautifully proportioned from an architectural point of view, a perfect example of an eighteenth century tavern; its interior likewise leaves little to be desired in a physical way, and has been well preserved. The building has necessarily undergone a succession of minor alterations; but essentially it is the same Flask it was in 1767.

If Highgate still preserves the definite air of being a village on the outskirts of the capital, Hampstead, with its famous Heath, does so possibly even more successfully. Hampstead has always conjured up in the minds of Londoners the vision of somewhere removed from grime. During the eighteenth century it was famous not merely as a place for recreation but also for its chalybeate springs, which when commercialised brought a good deal of affluence to the village community. Today it is a place where harassed Londoners may go for a stroll upon the Heath, or to inspect and admire the picturesque streets that abound here. It has however always been a fashionable residential district, serving those people who work in the greater London area but can afford to live at some little distance removed from their places of work and who today do not wish to join the ranks of conventional commuters. Rapid transportation is very much simpler to procure than a century or more ago, but even so Hampstead has succeeded in retaining the character of an outlying community, and although it has the letters N.W.3. affixed to its name for postal purposes it really is no part of London at all.

Literary and other personalities have always favoured Hampstead. The list is endless, but surely John Keats the poet is most celebrated of all. Painters have also come in large numbers, and in Holly Hill there once lived one of the finest of all English portrait painters, George Romney. In this same narrow street there is to be found one of the village's most picturesque taverns, appropriately called THE HOLLY BUSH. This fine building accords wholeheartedly with those surrounding it, and this is no mean compliment, for the residences in the immediate vicinity of this tavern are enviably attractive. Nearby Church Row is one of the most often photographed collections of private residences in the whole of London (and it should not be overlooked that the painter John Constable, who several times painted scenes on Hampstead Heath, is buried in the churchyard that lies at the end of Church Row, adding yet another lustrous name to those already associated with the village).

The Holly Bush has preserved virtually intact its old-fashioned, eighteenth century looks. Happily—for this is not always the case—the interior has remained as unchanged as the accession of electrically operated bar fittings will allow. Here are to be found small wood-panelled rooms in which it is possible to sit and discourse all evening if one so wishes, and with only a minimum of disturbance. It presents no hardship at all to imagine this pub a century and a half ago, populated by ardent poets, or journalists such as Leigh Hunt, arguing long over their latest creations and ambitions, or perhaps reflecting angrily over one of the frequent brushes with the law that were a characteristic of the hot-blooded Hunt's career.

The Holly Bush is an undoubted tourist attraction, a lovely place simply to look at; but in addition to this it is a first class public house, a local for many a Hampstead resident and a recommended place of retreat for the sightseer who may not find himself so ardent in the pursuit of novelty as he once thought he was. Slightly less obviously an attraction, but a famous "sight" even so, is THE SPANIARDS INN on Spaniards Road (N.W.3.), outside the village of Hampstead itself on the perimeter of the Heath.

Opposite this fine old inn stands a seventeenth century toll house, a firm reminder of the time when Hampstead really was an isolated community, not connected with the mass of Greater London in the way that it now is. It is not recorded exactly how long an inn has stood upon this site, but the present building dates from the eighteenth century, when its landlords were two brothers from Spain. It bore no fixed name then, and was known by the name of its landlords; because their names were difficult to pronounce the frequenters of the establishment quickly elected to refer to it as the Spaniards'.

The Holly Bush ..
HAMPSTEAD

Charles Dickens, who was as well acquainted with London's taverns as any man, naturally knew the Spaniards, with its low beams and sloping stone floors that are intact to this day. It was here that he caused Mrs. Bardell to take tea before she was arrested for costs in the breach of promise case she had unsuccessfully brought against Mr. Pickwick.

Dick Turpin also is reputed to have patronised this inn; and even today, in its sheltered rooms, it is easily possible to speculate about the muffled and sinister conversations that may at one time have been conducted in the shadows. Nor were such beings as Turpin the only miscreants to pause here: in 1780 the ill-directed Gordon rioters, with their futile cry of "no Popery", drank here to their wonted stage of intoxication before carrying on to burn down Lord Mansfield's residence nearby. Happily they were foiled, and the present pile, known as Kenwood House, is open to the public, who may there inspect the Iveagh Bequest, a fine collection of paintings and objets d'art, as well as some exquisite grounds. This show-place lies only a few minutes walk away from the Spaniards, and the visitor to one should not neglect to call in at the other.

The rioters' razing eventually came to an ignominious end. Today the Spaniards, although not tranquil—it is too popular for that—is a far more peaceful establishment than it was during those troubled times. Strollers on the Heath, even motorists (for alongside its fine garden where summer drinking is a much practised occupation it boasts that most unusual of London pub features, a car park), as well as local residents exchanging chatter about projected movies, plays or magazine articles, come here to sample the atmosphere of what is still essentially a village pub.

These then are just a few outlying pubs. London taverns, however, are predominantly those of the City and the west end, and it is necessary to return to more hectic thoroughfares in order to add to this selection. A pleasing way in which to begin is to pause in Shepherd's Market which, if anywhere in the west end deserves to be so recognised, does still seem a tiny hamlet—albeit a busy one—cut off from the rest of the west end, and even from the rest of Mayfair in which it lies.

Geographically, Shepherd's Market is the very heart of Mayfair, a little network of crowded narrow streets that are for the most part closed to motorised transport. This hidden-away warren of lanes houses a motley collection of small shops that range from butchers and bakers to antique dealers. In some ways an element of rurality still attaches itself to this colourful sector. The narrow thoroughfares lend a fervour to Shepherd's Market, a sense of hurry and confusion; they also add a touch of sprightliness to life that is sadly absent in so many areas of the capital city.

The sector is so named after an architect named Edward Shepherd, who owned this pocket of land as well as several other properties about Mayfair, and was established about 1735. It is therefore appropriate that the graceful tavern standing at the corner of Hertford Street (W.1.), with its delicately painted Regency blue and white exterior, should be named SHEPHERD'S. Shepherd himself, who died in 1747, was never of course the establishment's conductor, but he was the ground landlord.

Shepherd's exudes an atmosphere of gentility and luxury, quite in keeping with its situation and its eighteenth century background. Lovely wooden panelling graces its walls, while thick-piled carpets and comfortable seating add the finishing touches; and whereas it is pleasing upon occasions to sample the attractions of some of the more down-to-earth London taverns, it is equally enjoyable to walk into an essentially refined establishment such as this. It is difficult, seated in the lounge bar here, or in the comfortable restaurant upstairs, to recollect that during the tavern's early days, when the annual May Fair used to be held outside, and when the entire neighbourhood was abustle daily with market people and the area now embraced by Mayfair was a quite separate community from the west end—which meant the city of Westminster—public riot was the order of the day; that, and the squalor of waste food and other debris littered about the streets. Sedate Curzon Street, just a few yards away, affluent Park Lane, and of course the graceful tranquility of Shepherd's itself, lull one into forgetting this circumstance. But the facts remain, and those who are interested may easily unravel them.

Shepherds ~ ~ ~ SHEPHERD MARKET

Old Chesterfield ~
SHEPHERD STREET

Routstone 73

Since it has already been said that good pubs come in clusters, it is not surprising to find that tiny Shepherd's Market provides shelter for several very good establishments. THE OLD CHESTERFIELD in Shepherd Street (W.1.) may therefore be cited in addition to Shepherd's. This second tavern is named after the Earls of Chesterfield who once inhabited Chesterfield House at the corner of Curzon Street and South Audley Street. Alas, the house has now vanished, though the famous "Letters to his Son" of the fourth Earl, written from that address, have survived to amuse and instruct successive generations. The date over the restaurant attached to the Old Chesterfield is 1883, and this is a very fine late Victorian structure that accords admirably with its situation.

As well befits these environs, the Old Chesterfield within presents its customers with dignified and unostentatious luxury, not to mention a sedan chair converted into a telephone booth. Like the decor at nearby Shepherd's, that at the Old Chesterfield is also fittingly Regency in overall design, and the walls are wood-panelled in the same attractive way. Once again it is difficult to call to mind the rowdier Shepherd's Market of a couple of centuries earlier.

The Red Lion...
WAVERTON STREET

This is the Mayfair of a past age. All is changed, and this now most fashionable of areas, traffic congestion aside, is decorous in the extreme. At the very top of Charles Street, leading off Berkeley Square and running parallel to Curzon Street, stands a tavern that goes far to epitomise what one means when talking about a "Mayfair pub". This is THE RED LION, Waverton Street (W.1.).

Here certainly is one of Mayfair's most stylish and socially popular pubs, with spacious bars (including a doubles bar), a good dining area, an excellent cold buffet counter and pleasing decor that includes several fine paintings, both old and new. The Red Lion, like all the smaller taverns in this neighbourhood, would originally have been established to cater for the grooms and domestics serving fashionable private residences. Today many of those residences have gone, making way for large apartment blocks, while the residences of one-time grooms, as the section of Hays Mews directly opposite the Red Lion illustrates, have in their turn been handed over to people of fashion. It is these people, as well as those who work in the numerous offices in and around Berkeley Square, that today help to make the Red Lion one of the busiest pubs in the area.

Perhaps the pleasantest time of all to sample this excellent tavern is on a weekend during the summer, when drinkers crowd out of doors to sit at the tables provided in front of the Red Lion, or to stand in clusters and exchange gossip. The building is itself well-proportioned, typical of the latter half of the eighteenth century, and colourful sun shades above the windows only add to the attractiveness of its sheltered setting; a group of people standing at leisure about its diminutive cobbled forecourt completes the picture. But summer is not the only season of the year, and at any time this is a pub worthy of patronage, especially later on at night when the great majority of customers are local residents, not business people; then the atmosphere is one of a pleasing but refined informality.

The Punch Bowl
FARM STREET

If one passes along Waverton Street away from the Red Lion, crosses Hill Street and makes for Farm Street (W.1.), a matter of two minutes walk away, he will be rewarded in finding another excellent Mayfair tavern, one not quite so burdened by propriety perhaps as is the Red Lion, but a very fine and extremely popular establishment nonetheless. For here stands the unprepossessing looking PUNCH BOWL, a pub that makes no attempt at all to emblazon itself in order to attract new customers: it has no need to, for it already seems to cater for as many as it can cope with.

It is wonderfully situated. Farm Street, named after the old Hay Hill Farm upon whose ground this street is built, is graced by some lovely private residences. Alas, developers have pulled several of them down, and the Punch Bowl itself, standing at the upper end of the street, has surrendered its immediate neighbours in this way.

This tavern, too, dates from the eighteenth century and its low ceilings and darkened wood partitions precisely fit the image created in one's imagination of Georgian bibbers seated long over a steaming bowl of punch, clutching clay pipes between their teeth, and then in the small hours of the morning walking uncertainly home along the narrow cobbled streets that criss-crossed the neighbourhood. Many of them would have been military men, and appropriately there are guardsmen's helmets and antique weapons on display in the lounge. In the smaller snug there is in addition a fine little collection of old earthenware vats.

The Punch Bowl has withstood the insistent march of sophistication, and this in an area where independence of this kind must be difficult to support. It is all the better for it. Among its many incidental attractions is a separate buffet bar, where good food is to be procured. Both it and the Red Lion lie to the west of Berkeley Square, at the Park Lane end; on the other side of the square, nearer Bond Street, along an old mews, is yet another of Mayfair's tucked-away taverns, THE GUINEA in Bruton Place (W.1.), which lies just off the extreme north eastern corner of Berkeley Square. Nearer to the hub of business premises than the two houses just mentioned, the Guinea, or "Ye Olde One Pound One" as its name still officially is, naturally attracts a solid contingent of people who work nearby each day; but it also boasts many local residents among its regular patrons; and more important, it lies sufficiently hidden away to count among its devotees many a real connoisseur of London taverns. There is a further feature, and this must be mentioned even though it is not the purpose of this publication to advertise the products of any individual brewer: the Guinea is one of the dwindling number of west end taverns to serve the beer of one of the very few small independent breweries still active in London, a brew moreover that many drinkers consider to be the best available in the capital.

Bruton Place, which runs behind Bruton Street, is one more of those mews originally built to shelter the horses and grooms attached to the great houses that existed here in such abundance during the eighteenth and nineteenth centuries. Then, as now, Bruton Street was considered highly desirable and in it lived such men of fashion as the Duke of Argyll. It was in this street also, in 1809, that "Clemency" Canning lived. The Guinea can thus be dated with confidence to the last decades of the eighteenth century, although the wooden partitions and panelling that characterise it, now stained dark with age, are reminiscent of a slightly later date. The Guinea is a pub that is strictly devoid of gimmicks. It provides really excellent snack food at the bar, and it has some very fine old engravings hanging on the wall. That it lies almost literally only a stone's throw away from Bond Street, London's most exclusive shopping centre, bestows upon it a further valuable distinc-

The Guinea and
BRUTON PLACE

tion in the form of a praiseworthy lack of pretension. There is something of a Dickensian informality about the Guinea; a solidity also. It is a real pleasure to visit.

Leaving Mayfair and negotiating the furious thrust of traffic that now permanently distracts the stroller along Piccadilly, one enters another of London's quieter sectors, probably the most refined of all. For this is St. James', to whose court ambassadors from foreign countries are still accredited. This is also clubland, and one-time site of noble residences in almost overwhelming profusion. Just off St. James' Square, in Duke of York Street (S.W.I.), running south off Jermyn Street and adjacent to Wren's fine little church of St. James, Piccadilly, stands what is surely the London tavern with the widest-spread international reputation of them all. It goes under the fairly common name of THE RED LION, but there its ordinariness ends. There can be very few travel brochures distributed overseas that do not spotlight this excellent little establishment.

The reason for this, apart from the Red Lion's very real qualifications as a perfectly preserved late Victorian London tavern, is the magnificent display of hand engraved mirrors that cover the walls of what used to be the saloon bar. These mirrors constitute unquestionably the most photographed pub feature in all of London, and it is partly for this reason that, for a change, an illustration has been given here of the outside.

The Red Lion's facade is in truth an excellent example of a small London public house of the latter decades of the nineteenth century. The same may be said of almost every feature inside. Only one wooden partition remains now, but it is not difficult to imagine how this in any case quite small pub was once sub-divided into smaller rooms. The bar counter itself is a notable piece of work, with its irregularly curved design. It is gratifying how carefully this little pub has been nurtured and preserved over the years, and well it merits its far-flung reputation.

To the person who works in St. James' the physical appearance of a pub counts for a good deal less than it does for the stranger. He naturally

The Red Lion ---
DUKE OF YORK STREET

requires pleasant surroundings, but he also requires an adequate range of bar food for his lunchtime refreshment. Here the Red Lion surpasses almost any pub in the area. Space is limited, to say the least, and yet it is possible to order and eat at the bar a full-scale, freshly prepared hot luncheon ranging from the traditional sausage and mash to a plate full of roast beef and Yorkshire pudding with all the trimmings; and for those who do not wish a full lunch there is always an excellent range of hot and cold bar snacks.

If the word "charm" is to be applied to any London tavern this is a favoured candidate for the honour. It is a pity that the visitor is likely to come across it at a busy time, and if he wishes to inspect it in relative tranquility he would do well to keep in mind that here, as in other pubs, there are quieter times: between eleven and twelve in the morning for instance, or between seven and nine at night (never, however, on Sunday, for the Red Lion is closed then).

Red Lions seem to preponderate in St. James'. Passing back into St. James' Square, turning off into King Street to the right and walking along almost to St. James' Street, just off the left hand side of the road there is a narrow way known as Crown Passage (S.W.1.), and at the foot of it, almost in Pall Mall itself, stands a second RED LION, one moreover that insists upon being defined as a "country pub in town", with a "Village Lounge" upstairs to prove it.

The designation is far from being inappropriate: this Red Lion contrasts sharply with the grandeur of the Pall Mall clubs that lie at its doorstep, behind whose imposing facades slumber well wined and dined gentlemen of unimpeachable social credentials. Even its immediate setting, amid a small cluster of diminutive shops and cafes of variegated complexions, sets off its basically informal character to good effect. Were it not for the fact that after a pleasant lunchtime in the Red Lion it is necessary to pass into a neighbouring St. James' Street totally blocked with frustrated traffic it would almost be accurate to term this a country pub.

The lower portion of the premises is divided into three separate rooms, served from two entrances; while upstairs is a lounge and dining area. The interior is attractive, but the outer visage is most appealing: for this comparatively limited exterior has been carefully tended, its lower portion painted a delicate blue with hanging baskets highlighting what would otherwise be in danger of becoming an almost completely hidden-away

The Red Lion ...
CROWN PASSAGE

public house. Nor is it a particularly new structure, for it dates back at least to a time when gardens lay in front of the property, and in the original lease was a clause to the effect that the landlord must undertake to keep these gardens in good order. At that time there was a good deal of carefully tended open ground in this neighbourhood: all is now given over to large buildings. There is still a pleasant patch of green in the centre of St. James' Square, but this is private property. Fortunately St. James' Park, one of the most attractive in all London, is only three minutes walk away from Pall Mall. Its central lake and collection of exotic birds from all parts of the world are the delight of people who work in this part of London.

Across the park lies lovely Queen Anne's Gate, another little backwater of attractive residences that with the support of preservation orders should survive for many more years to come. Queen Anne's Mansions, a somewhat unimposing block of flats, has recently vanished however, to make room

Old Star & Crown
BROADWAY — Roulston 73

for an entirely new block designed by Sir Basil Spence. If the old mansions have gone, the pleasant tavern that must have served many of their occupants in its time, THE OLD STAR AND CROWN, Broadway (S.W.1.), thankfully remains, looking just as it has looked for many a year.

This recommended and very popular public house faces the imposing mass of the London Transport headquarters and convenient St. James' Park underground station. High up on its facade this latter building bears a series of large relief sculptures executed by the great Jacob Epstein, not much known, seldom regarded, and possibly of even greater interest to the curious for these two facts alone, but possessed of individual merit in any case and standing high among London's more contemporary public decorations.

58

Adjacent to the Old Star and Crown, running off Broadway, is Petty France. The street is worthy of mention because in a house that like all the others in the same place has fallen beneath bulldozers, John Milton wrote his epic poem of "Paradise Lost". Literary pilgrims might nevertheless like to walk along this now barely recognisable thoroughfare and make silent obeisance to the dead poet. If they do they may rest assured that a comfortable respite awaits them in the Old Star and Crown—a name deriving from its proximity to a nearby military establishment—after which they can quickly walk across to Westminster Abbey, but five minutes away, gained by way of Tothill Street (originally Toothill, supposedly denoting the highest point in the vicinity, though it is hard to credit the fact).

Civil servants stroll about St. James' Park during the lunch break; they also seem to provide the bulk of custom at the Old Star and Crown, where substantial bar snacks are provided. There is just one room here, with a central serving area; but it can easily be appreciated how not so very long ago this room was compartmentalised by means of wooden partitions, just as it would have been in the nineteenth century. Pressure of business and the democratic process have forced the disappearance of separate public and lounge bars. In almost every way this has been a beneficial trend, especially in a London tavern that is also a local, as this one is, where variety among the customers is always a welcome feature.

Passing west along Petty France, across Buckingham Gate and down a quiet little thoroughfare known as Wilfred Street (S.W.1.) there stands on a corner at the end of this street a tiny, little known public house that is among the gems of London taverns. THE CASK AND GLASS is such a diminutive establishment that patrons wishing to imbibe full pints of beer are discouraged: only half pint pots are provided, and in some ways this accords perfectly with the character of this most excellent pub.

The decor inside and out is praiseworthy. Wallpaper and furnishing are alike delicately tasteful, while the pavement immediately before this tavern is cluttered with a veritable miniature garden of flower boxes, which together with hanging baskets lend the Cask and Glass a welcoming appearance not only during the spring and summer months, but year round. Nor should the deceptively simple signboard of this fine tavern be overlooked: it is a credit to whoever secured its design, and easily among the most distinctive in London.

In some ways the Cask and Glass resembles a wine lodge as much as a pub: a wide range of sherries from the wood and wines by the glass is available here, and a single glass of chilled champagne is frequently to be procured, in itself an indication of the tavern's high standing. The range of spirits and liqueurs is also comprehensive. Indeed, in almost every way this is a perfect pub. The only regret the Londoner can have is the mass of deplorable high-rise buildings that in recent years have appeared outside its windows.

Happily the area immediately to the rear of the Cask and Glass has resisted all such molestation. Buckingham Place and Catherine Place, the two small streets immediately adjacent to Wilfred Street, harbour pleasing terraces of small, early nineteenth century houses. They appear almost as private residences still, though close inspection of the subdued brass plates on their doors reveals that they are in truth the offices of engineering consultants, architects, accountants and other professional people, who are all enabled to conduct their businesses in relative quiet only a few minutes walk away from the bustle of Victoria mainline railway station. These people provide the Cask and Glass with a steady stream of custom.

It is close also to Buckingham Palace, and sightseers who do not care for the brashness of larger public houses may like to keep it in mind. However, it must not be allowed to go unsaid that the Cask and Glass lies in a part of London quite densely provided with public houses, and although it happens to be one of the more unusual pubs in the area, and good by any standards, it is not perhaps the place for the "hearty" rugger-playing swiller of beer, nor is it the ideal venue for a raucous office party, and such prospective patrons might be better advised to select an alternative tavern.

Leaving the area about Victoria, it is necessary to return to the west end of town. If Trafalgar Square and Leicester Square provide two focal points, either of them second only to Piccadilly Circus itself, then a pub lying half way between the two of them, especially if it is a good one, is bound to be of interest to the tavern enthusiast. Such a pub exists in the form of THE HAND AND RACQUET in Whitcomb Street (W.C.2.).

The narrow and colourful little thoroughfare in which it lies, with its collection of small shops and sandwich bars, was known originally as Hedge Lane, but it has borne its present name at least since 1677, and some of the

Cask & Glass —
WILFRED STREET

buildings still standing there date from the late seventeenth century. The name of the Hand and Racquet derives from its proximity to the Royal Tennis Court that was once situated nearby and was much resorted to by King Charles II. This court survived until well into the nineteenth century, but today its site is covered over and only the name of this tavern stands as a positive testimony to its one-time existence.

There is a Dickensian flavour about Whitcomb Street, and this agreeable and gaily painted Victorian structure graces it admirably. The interior also is attractively decorated; but perhaps the old-time atmosphere is best sampled in the upstairs restaurant, where business lunches are served during the week, where beer still has to be brought up by the glass from downstairs and the food is strictly of a traditional English kind. There is a good deal of warmth to be experienced here, warmth being an example of one of the good London tavern's special properties.

Trafalgar Square was not laid out until the 1830's. Before that time the area it now covers was taken up by the King's, or Royal Mews, so called because at one time the royal falcons used to be kept there. Horsemanship was also practised in the mews, and during the latter half of the eighteenth century a famous menagerie that used to be put on display at the Exeter Exchange in the nearby Strand was also based here. The mews was finally taken down in 1830, exactly thirty years before the Hand and Racquet was built.

Thus old London continually makes way for new London, while little pockets such as one side of Whitcomb Street remain unharmed. One ought to be thankful for the juxtaposition of old and new, for they complement one another and oblige people to take notice of them. Soho, another village community that has been engorged for more than two centuries now within the mass of greater London, allows this opportunity perhaps better than anywhere outside the City of London itself, for it mingles the continual bustle of contemporary life with the very firm reminders of bygone days that its narrow streets, huddled buildings and multifarious commercial headquarters seem somehow to highlight. That there are several very good taverns in Soho comes as no surprise.

THE WHITE HORSE in Rupert Street (W.1.), just off Shaftesbury

The Hand & Racquet

WHITCOMB STREET

Avenue, is one of them. Much patronised by members of the acting profession, it lies in the heart of theatreland. And if there is one London pub that may be termed a theatrical pub, not merely one that boasts past connections with the theatre, then possibly it is the White Horse. Actresses and actors, famous and forlorn, as well as a host of backstage personnel, are to be found here at all times, and fittingly there are numerous theatrical photographs about the walls, as well as a "Theatre Bar" upstairs.

Two minutes walk away from Regent Street and Piccadilly Circus, this tucked-away tavern with its excellent cold buffet counter and its provision for full hot luncheons during the week is obviously a convenient establishment in its own right. It boasts another great advantage however, as a glance along Rupert Street at any time of the day, as well as along adjoining Berwick Street, will immediately reveal. For here is established one of central London's finest open-air markets. Stalls selling cut-price gramophone records and suchlike are to be discovered along Berwick Street, while in Rupert Street there is even a waggon-load of second hand books;

The White Horse ~ ~ ~
RUPERT STREET

but basically this is a fruit and vegetable market, one of the centres of trade of the anciently established fraternity of London costermongers—though they no longer go under that name, and undoubtedly they enjoy a greater measure of affluence than did their counterparts who operated in London in their thousands during the nineteenth century. Some of London's finest continental food shops are to be discovered in nearby Brewer Street and Old Compton Street, and this open-air market complements them admirably.

Curiously, during the nineteenth century the costermongers accounted for a large proportion of popular theatre audiences, and they are recorded as enjoying not only "blood and thunder" melodramas but even Shakespeare—though some of the soliloquies apparently encouraged yawns—and so it is fitting that this market should be situated so securely in theatreland. As far as the White Horse is concerned, fruit sellers mingle with stage personalities in pleasing harmony and bestow upon the establishment a genuine warmth that exhibits London, and its lighter side, to splendid advantage.

It is of course an inescapable truism that Soho has earned itself an unsavoury reputation for qualities far divergent from what this publication is intended to broadcast. To the Londoner, though, these less attractive aspects are insignificant: to him the name of Soho conveys a reminder of the wonderful concentration of good food shops and first class restaurants to be unearthed there; while to the historian of London the name of Soho means an almost "lost" portion of the metropolis, but one that still abounds in antique memorials.

Poland Street (W.1.), which runs due south off Oxford Street down as far as Broadwick Street, harbours its fair share of historical associations. Here Dr. Burney the great musician was living in 1760, together with his young daughter Fanny, who later became the celebrated Madame d'Arblay. A street running east off Poland Street is today named after this famous lady of letters. In Poland Street also lived the poet, painter and mystic, William Blake. And it is in this street that the second tavern in Soho chosen for inclusion in these pages is to be found, THE STAR AND GARTER.

This is a small pub, with an exterior that immediately betokens its eighteenth century origins, even though definite records extend no further back in time than to 1825; but the facade is a little deceptive, for within there is an upstairs restaurant where lunchtime grills are a speciality during the week, in addition to the ground floor bar area. A measure of the Star and Garter's authentic antiquity is displayed in the show of old clay pipes and coins that were actually discovered on the premises when it was being altered some few years ago, and which stand beside a fine display of other miscellaneous curios, including African weapons. This apart, the establishment still allows a taste of yesteryear, and in an age when so many other reminders of a London that cannot fend for itself are disappearing beneath the bulldozer's wrathful advance virtually wholesale, this, to the resident, is of paramount importance.

A minute or two's walk from the rush of Oxford Street, in the heart of an area dense with different business houses, obviously the Star and Garter caters for a considerable trade from these quarters. It is also a "local" and it is in addition the kind of pub just slightly removed from the busier thoroughfares that evening strollers delight to call at, perhaps to linger in the amusingly named "Smoochy Bar". Nor will casual visitors be disappointed: this is an excellent little tavern, one that gives as vivid an impression of what a London pub really is as any other it is possible to name. That it also boasts a respectable pedigree and lies in the centre of an area welling with historical interest merely heightens its attractiveness.

Star & Garter
POLAND STREET

Chapter Three

This third chapter, after a glance at a few remaining west end taverns, spreads into the City of London itself, that part of the capital best known to Dr. Johnson. It also spreads south of the Thames in a couple of instances. But before glancing at some City taverns it is rewarding to look at one or two that lie just beyond its western reaches, and there is no finer establishment with which to begin than THE LAMB AND FLAG in Rose Street (W.C.2.), a lovely pub to look at both inside and out, and a most satisfying place at which to pause.

Its situation lends the Lamb and Flag one of its principal assets, for it stands at the head of a narrow lane leading off Garrick Street, which in itself hints at the past theatrical associations of this 400 years old tavern (though the present building is not itself quite that old); while some old playbills and theatrical engravings about the walls testify to the aptness of this claim. More to the point, this pub has always boasted active stage connections, and still does so in the form of providing space for the presentation of live plays at certain times of the year, usually at lunchtime.

During the sixteenth and seventeenth centuries popular plays were commonly given in inns and inn-yards, and the admixture of spectacle with liquorous bonhomie worked to good effect. The practice has alas all but died out, and it is thus more than encouraging to come across a contemporary tavern still involved in dramatic productions in this way; and especially when the tavern in question is such a delightful structure as is the Lamb and Flag.

Rose Street was once more accurately called Rose Alley, at a time when it extended much further than does the present thoroughfare. That was a considerable time ago: "Red Rose Street, 1623", read the sign over one house until it was demolished in 1859 to make way for Garrick Street. During the eighteenth century Rose Street was renowned for its squalor and the overcrowding of the dwellings that lined it. Debauchery of one kind or another was the keynote, and gambling and cockfighting were the two most popular distractions. The Lamb and Flag, as may be well imagined, was an important centre for both cockfighting and prizefighting throughout those less genteel years.

It also acted incidentally as a setting for plentiful violence of another kind, at a time when street drubbing was a common occurrence. One doleful September evening during 1679 the Poet Laureate, John Dryden, was attacked and beaten just outside the Lamb and Flag on account of some satirical lines he had written about Charles II's mistress. Poor Dryden, three months later, on December 18, he suffered similar treatment, again in Rose Street, at the instigation of the Earl of Rochester, because of some lines falsely attributed to him. This second attack occurred after he had left Wills' Coffee House in nearby Bow Street.

Rose Street provided refuge for Samuel Butler, author of "Hudibras", who died here; it also drew the attentions of Charles Dickens, who is said to have patronised the Lamb and Flag by no means infrequently. Happily it remains as a perfect gem of an early London tavern; and if the original street is no more, at least this pub with its attractive frontage and its old-world interior that seems to have altered but little over the past two centuries is a solid reminder of a now vanished age.

In nearby Monmouth Street (W.C.2.), which extends in a northerly direction off St. Martin's Lane, there stands another worthwhile tavern that the enthusiast should not overlook. This is THE TWO BREWERS, one more pub with very real theatrical connections, boasting numerous autographed photographs of stage personalities about its walls. However, stage people and their professional aides and associates in no way make up the entire body of the clientele of this attractive little pub with its plentiful array of bar food. It stands amid numerous offices and other places of work, and conducts a brisk trade from the people connected with them. It is to be confidently recommended both for its comfort and for the standard of its catering.

The Two Brewers was not in existence at the time when Dickens wrote his well known "Meditations on Monmouth Street", one of the "Sketches by Boz". The street he then described was one given over mainly to the sale of second–hand clothes. But before Dickens' time this narrow street had enjoyed a reputation for being a most fashionable and genteel place in which to purchase clothing. Neither image fits it today; though it is true that it is lined on both sides by some very curious and quaint shops, and

The Lamb & Flag
ROSE STREET

one or two of them sell clothing. However, Monmouth Street does cling to a distinctly Dickensian flavour, which is in turn abetted by the presence of several premises housing what may be termed the backroom departments of theatrical life—wig makers, costumiers, make-up manufacturers—and this tavern nestles agreeably among them.

To find a neighbouring establishment of merit it is necessary to step from Monmouth Street only as far as New Row (W.C.2.), which lies just off St. Martin's Lane in the direction of Covent Garden. Hereabouts were once the Bermudas, a maze of obscure little alleys renowned for their unwholesomeness, of which perhaps the most curiously named of all was Porridge Island, so called because of the great preponderance of inexpensive cook shops that used to line it. The whole area was cleared about 1829, in the reforms that preceded the laying out of Trafalgar Square nearby. There are still narrow streets in plenty, however, and numerous eating establishments; while a most attractive little tavern, THE WHITE SWAN, lies decorously among them.

Two Brewers . . .
MONMOUTH STREET

This house's most unusual feature is its wine bar, a separate room in which only wines and spirits are dispensed—at least in theory, for beer drinkers wander in through the open door from the main bar. A wide range of wines is provided, and there is always a special "wine of the day" on sale. But naturally there is a good deal more to the pub than this, otherwise it would not qualify for inclusion here. Good bar food is available, and there is a large bar with plentiful seating for non-wine drinkers.

The White Swan lies in theatrical territory and enjoys the patronage of both players and playgoers; but it is also on the fringe of Covent Garden and as a result, as can be well imagined,

The White Swan
NEW ROW

benefits from the patronage of a whole myriad of people. If it is this that constitutes one essential element for establishing an enjoyable public house then the White Swan may certainly claim attention. Its attractive exterior and colourful signboard, as well as a most successful renovation within, also play important roles, and they have helped to make this tavern an extremely popular establishment.

There are three more taverns, lying somewhat to the north of those just recommended, that are also worthy of mention. The first is THE NEWMAN ARMS in Rathbone Street (W.C.1.), another of London's tiny taverns, lying beside a narrow alleyway that runs between Newman Street and Rathbone Street, both of which themselves run north off Oxford Street at its Tottenham Court Road extreme.

The Newman Arms, more particularly during the less crowded hours of business, allows the imagination a vivid glimpse of nineteenth century London: of men puffing dedicatedly at evil-smelling pipes, pausing long over their glasses of thick black porter or their quarterns of murderous gin, seated at bare wooden tables in a dimly illuminated room.

There was nothing particularly admirable about such a circumstance. Often enough, drunkenness went hand in hand with poverty: long hours passed in pubs for want of anywhere else more comfortable to sit inevitably resulted in drunkenness. Nevertheless, the pubman of our own day likes to indulge in at least the nostalgic exercise of casting a backward glance towards such times, patronising the little public houses that infested the metropolis; and if such down-to-earth, spit-and-sawdust places no longer exist it is at least rewarding to chance upon one that could possibly at one time have been such a place—however erroneous the supposition, for certainly the Newman Arms is not so today—and which affords the opportunity to delve mentally back in time a little.

Low ceilings, darkened walls and two small rooms sum up the Newman Arms. The very smallness of the establishment highlights what is almost an air of intimacy; and if the term Dickensian, as it is usually applied, may be accorded to any London tavern unreservedly then the Newman Arms claims particular precedence. Was it not in Newman Street, a half minute's walk away through the little side alley, that Mr. Turveydrop of "Bleak House" kept a dancing academy "in a sufficiently dingy house at the corner of an archway with busts in all the staircase windows"? Newman Street still presents many a mean looking structure, and it is an easy matter to imagine characters from Dickens' pages stepping from them and making their way through the narrow passage just mentioned and into the Newman Arms, where warmth, contentment and companionship were to be secured for only a few coppers.

The Newman Arms ~~~
RATHBONE STREET

During the eighteenth century the area immediately to the west of this spot boasted a good deal of spaciousness and open ground, allowing the existence of such places of distraction as Marylebone Gardens. These stood at the heart of a most graceful sector of London, among the great squares, then newly founded, that today provide the capital with some of its best memorials of their age. Within St. Marylebone there are numerous fine public houses, yet the one selected here, in Marylebone High Street (W.1.), on the corner of Nottingham Street, is of a high Victorian character, redolent of earlier date in name only. This tavern lies a little outside the limits embraced by this chapter, but it demands mention and is therefore included here.

For no very good reason, since it demonstrably dates from the 1870's or thereabouts, it bears the name of THE PRINCE REGENT, and a mural on the wall inside presents a full length portrait of the prince. Delicately contrived decor heightens the Regency theme of this establishment, but essentially it is a Victorian pub, one of several that exist close by, and among the finest looking in all London of its own period and kind. And even apart from its far from negligible value as a curio on this account, the Prince Regent may claim the attention of the twentieth century Londoner for its general excellence as a public house, where comfort, good bar food, an attractive restaurant and a buffet counter are among its qualifications.

It has been well preserved outside, and looks little different from what it must have looked a century ago. The interior too is pleasingly decorated, with supporting pillars about the bar counter fashioned in the shape of Moorish figures. In addition, there is a fine collection of old cheese dishes on display. The whole establishment exudes a feeling of lushness; no student of Victorian London should miss it, or for that matter the entire neighbourhood, that for some curious reason, perhaps because it is not often visited by tourists, has managed to survive in a quite surprising semblance of its original state, chequered by perpetual reminders of a more gracious "age of reason" that preceded the erection of this tavern by a full century.

The Prince Regent
MARYLEBONE HIGH STREET

The Prince Regent stands in a somewhat isolated position in relation to the other centrally situated public houses mentioned in these pages, and perhaps THE MUSEUM TAVERN in Great Russell Street (W.C.1.) may be more convenient for those who wish merely to inspect a typical Victorian public house. Few visitors to London can fail to observe this establishment, for, as its name suggests, it stands directly opposite the British Museum.

To scholars from all over the world who visit the museum in the course of their professional exertions the name of this tavern has always meant the place to which they might resort for casual refreshment after their labours in the British Museum reading room (itself graced by the largest dome in London and by no means a negligible architectural phenomenon). The lease of the Museum Tavern dates from 1854, the year in which what was then Montague House was acquired for the nation to be converted into a museum. To many this might appear quite an ordinary pub, praiseworthy for its provision of a good array of food, served both from the bar and at table, but to many more it represents what can only be termed a tradition.

Readers from the British Museum, who might have to wait an hour or more for the delivery of precious tomes to their desks, come here to while away the annoying minutes; publishers and their editors, who exist in abundance within the immediate vicinity, flood here at lunchtime and again as soon as they leave off work in the evening; and it has even been known for better-off authors to dictate to their secretaries inside this very pub. There is thus to be detected here the presence of a London or even an international intelligentsia of scholars, professional writers and those concerned with marketing the written word. Fortunately the Museum Tavern is also a local public house, catering to a wide cross-section of the community, and perhaps because of this it has always avoided transformation into an exclusive haunt of the habitués of the British Museum.

A useful partition that used to separate public bar from saloon has vanished in recent years, and with it just a little of the nineteenth century bouquet that indisputably hangs over this tavern. What remains however is a magnificent serving counter behind the bar, with ornate carved woodwork and ornamental mirrors that, as more and more older taverns are either demolished or severely renovated, must surely be extremely rare. Such splendid appurtenances as this are deserving of admiration, if only because that is the most certain way of securing their continued employment. This apart, it is surely worthwhile taking notice of articles that were originally contrived only with the application of considerable care and patience, not at the whim of a machine producing standardised fittings for a chain of public houses under the same ownership.

A very few minutes walk away from the Museum Tavern leads one into the Aldwych, the western end of Fleet Street and the outskirts of the City of

Museum Tavern
GT. RUSSELL STREET

London, where pubs have taken to themselves a character that, although in no way uniform, is immediately recognisable as different from that, of the average west end tavern, even if it is not quite as definable. Much of this is due to the kind of work City men carry out: journalism, finance, the administration of the law; but much stems from a very real awareness on the part of almost everybody connected with the City that in point of seniority it takes precedence over other areas of London. Not only that, it is an uncompromising fact also that London's two best-remembered literary worthies, Johnson and Dickens, can be associated with the City in most distinct terms. Further, some of the finest architecture in the whole of London, both domestic and ecclesiastical, is to be discovered here; so, incongruously, are some of London's most lovely little nooks and crannies. That really good taverns abound is therefore hardly surprising.

The first of these is THE SEVEN STARS, Carey Street (W.C.2.), a pub that for many years has been much patronised by members of the legal

profession. Apart from being the smallest of all the legal pubs, it is also one of the most praiseworthy. It stands just to the rear of the Law Courts, off Chancery Lane and close to Lincoln's Inn Fields, thereby commanding a highly convenient and enviable situation. There is a distinctly unusual feature about the Seven Stars in that it claims to have been erected, as it now stands, as long ago as 1602—which suggests that it was one of the few City taverns to escape the Great Fire of 1666—and this fact alone naturally gives it something of an antiquarian attraction. The fact that its walls are covered with numerous old engravings and cartoons of the house itself, its environs and the many legal luminaries who have frequented it over the decades also lends it a creditable distinction.

The patrons of this small, low-ceilinged old pub demand good food and good wine, and they receive them both; and in this of course lies the Seven Stars' principal claim to patronage in the London of today. But it also has certain other claims on the pubman's attention, not the least of which is its unusual name. It was originally called the "Leg and Seven Stars", a corruption of the "League and Seven Stars", an allusion to the United Provinces of the Netherlands.

This is not all. There are Dickensians who will still aver that the Seven Stars provided the original for the "Magpie and Stump" in "Pickwick Papers". But actually the Dickens creation, although certainly based upon a particular pub, lay at the corner of nearby Portugal Street, and would probably have been either the "George IV Tavern" or the "Black Jack Tavern" that stood next to one another in that street. It is always a pity to diverge from legends of this kind, but general opinion certainly holds that the Seven Stars was not the tavern Dickens had in mind in this instance— although he would of course have been well acquainted with it.

Lincoln's Inn Fields provide one of the particular attractions of this sector of London, not least because of the quietude that seems to pervade them. This was not always the case: in the early eighteenth century the sometimes rowdy Lincoln's Inn Fields Theatre stood here, principal competitor of Drury Lane Theatre and predecessor of Covent Garden Theatre which opened its doors in 1732. Earlier still, until about the reign of Queen Elizabeth I, these "Fields" really were fields, and one of them, Fichett's Field, lay between what are now Portugal Street, Carey Street and Searle Street. If the date of origin attributed to the Seven Stars is correct—and why should it not be so?—it must have been erected at the very time when this part of the capital was beginning its development in earnest. That it survives as a memento of these early days is a matter for congratulation.

Two minutes walk away, across what is the very tail end of the Strand, lie two old London taverns of eighteenth century vintage, literally within a few moments walk of one another, that bear names in honour of one and the same person. They are THE ESSEX HEAD in Essex Street (W.C.2.) and THE DEVEREUX in Essex Court (E.C.4.), and they take their name from Robert Devereux, first Earl of Essex and favourite of Queen Elizabeth I, whose residence was situated on ground now occupied by these two taverns and other buildings in the same complex. The Devereux carries a stone-carved bust of the famous Earl high up on its facade, while the Essex Head boasts three attractive cameos colourfully painted on its outer walls at ground floor level. Both taverns possess interesting past associations, and both lie within only a few yards of the Temple, where for several centuries chambers have been provided for members of the legal profession; though originally this was the site of the monastic headquarters of the Knights Templar. Dr. Johnson lived for a while in a house now supplanted by Dr. Johnson's Buildings and it is easy to imagine the philosopher-lexicographer stepping out of an evening to either of these two taverns—as indeed he did.

The Temple is one of the loveliest spots in all of London, enveloped by peacefulness and yet only a minute away from Fleet Street. It is gracious in character, crowded with fine old buildings and gardens. Charles Lamb was born in Crown Office Row here in 1795. He was the author of the famous "Essays of Elia", and as everybody knows he was a prodigious drinker—not to say drunkard, even by his own confession—and he too would have been well aware of these two fine City taverns.

It was at the Essex Head in 1783 that Dr. Johnson founded the Essex Head Club; though the tavern was then more familiarly known as Sam's, after the name of its landlord Samuel Greaves. Many members of Johnson's circle came here to talk of literary matters on three evenings a week. A fine of twopence (quickly raised to threepence) was levied on every member who failed to attend a meeting. This was one of the last literary assemblies presided over by Johnson, but it is by no means of diminished interest because of that.

Since those days the Essex Head has kept up to date with passing require-ments until today it is a very attractive tavern both inside and out, fitting decorously into its snug setting. During the evening, perhaps because it is smaller than its rival a few yards away, it is an altogether quieter establish-

The Essex Head ~~
ESSEX STREET

F

ment in which to pass away idle minutes in conversation.

The Devereux is the legal tavern to surpass all others, and has been known for its legal associations for many decades now; indeed, so closely is it associated with the individuals who exert themselves professionally in the Law Courts every day, as well as those whose job it is to report the happenings there, the daily "Cause List" is displayed in the bar itself. But the Devereux is not without another history, for throughout the eighteenth century, indeed right through until 1843 when it closed, it was the well known Grecian Coffee House, which derived its name from its original Greek owner.

The Grecian was one of the most celebrated coffee houses in

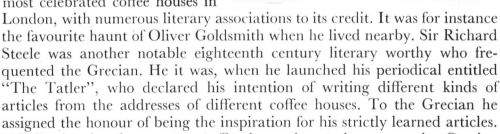

The Devereux ~ ~ ~
ESSEX COURT

Roulstone 73

London, with numerous literary associations to its credit. It was for instance the favourite haunt of Oliver Goldsmith when he lived nearby. Sir Richard Steele was another notable eighteenth century literary worthy who frequented the Grecian. He it was, when he launched his periodical entitled "The Tatler", who declared his intention of writing different kinds of articles from the addresses of different coffee houses. To the Grecian he assigned the honour of being the inspiration for his strictly learned articles.

Following its closure as a coffee house it was known as the Grecian Chambers, but it quickly became a pub and today is a City tavern par excellence. It has two large bars, well stocked to cater to legal palates, and is crowded at most times. The greatest satisfaction is to be derived from observing the unsanctimonious countenances of members of the judiciary during their moments of respite in the Devereux.

Upstairs is a grill room, which has always enjoyed a high reputation for its traditional chops and beefsteaks, served in civilised surroundings. This obviously provides the Devereux with one of its major attractions, but one other attraction that is not essentially of the building itself stems from its location. The area immediately surrounding the Devereux and the Essex Head is a part of the City that the tourist so often misses, with its maze of little courts and side streets, speckled with excellent taverns and wine houses, and some exquisite little churches, as well as numerous unexpected private residences. These are the factors that help to make the City something a good deal in excess of a mere centre of commerce, and taverns such as those just described undeniably play their part in adding to its attractiveness.

Red Lion Court (E.C.4.) lies some short distance away, off the north side of Fleet Street, the second alleyway from Fetter Lane travelling east. Hidden away up this narrow thoroughfare is another delightful City pub, THE RED LION TAVERN, after which the court itself is named and which, in a different outward guise, was certainly in existence as early as 1571.

A sixteenth century manuscript preserved in the British Museum lists all the taverns and "ordinaries" to be encountered along the route from Whitehall into the City of London. It is a prodigious list, for the Londoner of Shakespeare's day was far better provided with drinking places than is his counterpart of the twentieth century. Among the names is a Red Lion, which may or may not have been the one sited in Red Lion Court, but, as has been seen, it was in existence at that time, and it seems fair to assume that it would have been included in any such list.

Literary associations may be adduced here almost as it were by proxy. Nearby is Johnson's Court, named not after the illustrious writer but after Thomas Johnson, a late sixteenth century merchant, but also lived in at one time by Dr. Johnson. Later, during the early nineteenth century, Samuel Taylor Coleridge the poet gave a series of lectures on Shakespeare in a building in Crane Court, which stands next to Red Lion Court. But surely the literary connections of the Red Lion today, as for many decades past, revolve about its proximity to so many Fleet Street newspaper offices. In many ways this Red Lion is the favourite retreat of journalists, and this

Red Lion Tavern
RED LION COURT

today is one of its principal claims to fame.

From the outside it appears only a very small tavern; yet appearances are deceptive, for the lounge bar is surprisingly spacious, and even more surprising is the first class restaurant to be discovered upstairs, so popular with regular patrons. In a nutshell, apart from allowing the stranger a glimpse of the extra-mural aspect of Fleet Street life, the Red Lion is a thoroughly capable and well conducted establishment and has been for many years.

The present building does not of course date from the sixteenth century. It is, rather, a pleasant brick structure that accords admirably with its slightly hidden-away position. The London of the eighteenth century, of Dr. Johnson, is still discernible here in subdued but immediately visible colours, and if the offices of the famous publisher Nichols, which stood in Red Lion Court until 1808 when they were destroyed by fire, are no more, there are still plenty of hints of the literary past.

The name of Johnson appears in connection with the taverns of this area seemingly out of all proportion to his present popularity as a writer—for he is more read about than read. But the truth is he was such a noteworthy tavern frequenter that it is difficult to find any good pub still standing in that part of the City where he lived that he did not visit. He lived in nearby Bolt Court during the latter years of his life—at a time admittedly when he did not allow himself to drink too copiously any longer for reasons of health—and he would certainly have known the Red Lion. He also knew the famous OLDE CHESHIRE CHEESE of course, situated in the aptly named Wine Office Court (E.C.4.), and to many people, Londoners and strangers alike, this is the one tavern with which the lexicographer's name is inescapably linked.

Ye Olde Cheshire Cheese ~~
WINE OFFICE COURT

How tantalising, therefore, to find that there is but slim substantiation for asserting that Johnson definitely frequented the Cheshire Cheese—even if it is hard to believe he did not do so. Johnson's great contemporary and close acquaintance, Oliver Goldsmith, lived for a time in this very court, and it is inconceivable that at some time he and Johnson did not sup here together; it is simply that there is no record of the fact. As though to bring the point home, the Cheshire Cheese today proudly displays in one of its rooms what is justly claimed to be "Dr. Johnson's Chair". That it was actually removed from another public house nearby, the old "Mitre Tavern", seems hardly to matter at all: a copy of Sir Joshua Reynolds' famous portrait of Johnson graces the walls of the same room, and truly the doctor's shade seems to inhabit the place.

This of course arises not so much from the fact that Johnson may have been a patron at one time as from the fact that the Cheshire Cheese presents one with a perfectly preserved example of the eighteenth century City tavern. Like most other buildings in the neighbourhood, this tavern perished during the Great Fire of 1666; but the rebuilding dates from 1667, and it seems hardly to have altered at all since that date, apart from the introduction over the years of the latest aids to dispensing drink and serving food. And little Wine Office Court is a delightful nook of olden times, just removed from Fleet Street and the hubbub of that busy thoroughfare. Deep-stained walls, low ceilings and a number of small-proportioned rooms both upstairs and down characterise this tavern, not to mention floors sprinkled with sawdust; but the Cheshire Cheese, in addition to being a unique tourist attraction, is an efficiently functioning City pub, and it is much favoured by people who work nearby.

The great pudding that used to be prepared and served here well into the twentieth century drew numerous patrons: it weighed between fifty and eighty pounds and was prepared in one huge basin, topped by a light crust. Although this famous pudding was never served during Johnson's day he is often presented in the annals of imagination as partaking of it; but chops and beefsteak would have been the customary fare here in his day. The pudding season used to begin on the first Monday in October, when a distinguished guest would be invited to make the first cut; its contents, cooked to a secret recipe, included not only whole steaks and kidneys, but oysters, larks, mushrooms and many other ingredients that fairly make the mouth water.

Good food is still served in the Cheshire Cheese's excellent restaurant (and strangers should be warned that there is more than one tavern of this name in central London). Numerous curios and old prints are preserved about the walls of this recommended City tavern, one that eschews pretentiousness and in so doing happily retains a genuine sense of a London that has seemingly vanished for ever.

Fortunately there are a few other reminders of the City of yesteryear. Carrying on eastwards from the Cheshire Cheese, down to the bottom of Fleet Street and across Ludgate Circus into Ludgate Street, one of the first turnings leading off to the left is the notorious Old Bailey (E.C.4.), home of the Central Criminal Court and setting for celebrated trials almost beyond count. Even today it is impossible to pass by this formidable structure without a shudder, and by good fortune there is immediately to hand one of the best pubs in the City, the aptly named MAGPIE AND STUMP, which as has already been hinted is in no way connected with the tavern of Charles Dickens' imagination that went under the same name.

Yet even this well known tavern conceals barbarous skeletons within its cupboards. Newgate Prison used to stand nearby, and the Magpie and Stump stands directly opposite the spot where public executions used once to take place, following Tyburn Tree's becoming defunct in 1783. Successive landlords drew good money from renting rooms so that those interested might obtain an unobstructed view of the butchery beneath—which delights, until 1789, included burning at the stake as well as hanging. An indication of the immense popularity of these unruly spectacles is to be drawn from the fact that when in 1864 the train killer Franz Müller was executed here some 50,000 people crowded about Old Bailey to witness his final disgrace. At about this time also James Payn, later an eminent

journalist, paid as much as twenty guineas to witness an execution from the windows of the Magpie and Stump. By 1868 the whole proceedings had taken on such scandalous proportions that all subsequent executions took place within the prison walls.

This tavern dates back to the eighteenth century, and although for a while its name was changed to the "King of Denmark", the original nomenclature was finally restored. Traditionally a magpie is a symbol of good tidings, and so perhaps it was only right and proper that when public executions took place nearby the symbol should be removed. And in case mention of all these gory past practices should serve to deter the potential visitor, it has to be stressed that this pub today is an extremely civilised institution, patronised by a widely varied clientele and well deserving of a visit.

Magpie & Stump ~ ~

OLD BAILEY

R.

For the visitor St. Paul's Cathedral standing close by is the primary architectural attraction, but for the curio hunter, if he is willing to walk a little way, there stands beneath the Blackfriars railway bridge, in Queen Victoria Street (E.C.4.), one of those eccentricities of pub architecture that never cease to prompt wonder and admiration and that surely far surpasses in its inventiveness any of the "theme" pubs of recent years. It is of course THE BLACK FRIAR, next door to the new Times Building, across the road from the Mermaid Theatre and within two minutes walk of the banks of the Thames.

From the outside this tavern appears but a gaunt and perhaps slightly over-ornate late Victorian structure, adorned by reasonably unusual features but otherwise hardly deserving of a special visit. It is only inside that the true uniqueness of the place becomes apparent, for there, all is marble mosaic and intricately fashioned woodwork that mingle the influence of the English Arts and Crafts Movement of the second half of the nineteenth century with the *art nouveau* style that so preoccupied *fin de siecle* designers and that today is all the fashion once again.

Until quite recent times it was usual to talk about the "bad taste" manifested in decorative work of this kind; but for the time being at any rate one is allowed publicly to admire it. Whether one totally approves of the decor at the Black Friar or not it would be impossible to deny both its functional purpose in providing a public house with a very individual atmosphere and the high level of very careful workmanship shown in the carvings of jovial friars, the mosaic mottos set into the walls and the delicately fashioned bar fittings, pillars and alcoves.

A very small room separated from the main room by an archway possesses a curved mosaic ceiling that veritably causes it to resemble a miniature Byzantine mosque. The mottos about the walls are redolent of the publicly expressed ideals of the era in which it was created: "Haste is Slow", "Finery is Foolery", "Industry is All". Emerging from this recess it comes as no surprise to discover that the few lights burning immediately about the main fireplace are all gas powered.

As with the immediate neighbourhood from which it takes its name, the Black Friar stands about the site of what was at one time a Dominican priory, whose inhabitants were dressed in black (as opposed to the white assumed by the Carmelites established at nearby Whitefriars) and who were established here as early as 1276. As a City pub it is well known and widely patronised; and one particular advantage it has, possibly arising from its close proximity to a newspaper office, is that it remains open throughout the evening, as opposed to a number of houses in the vicinity which, the business people having departed, close their doors quite early on.

Moving over to the more easterly reaches of the City, just off Fenchurch Street, in Hart Street (E.C.3.), stands a public house that, from the outside at any rate, seems in some way to complement the Black Friar. This is THE SHIP, formerly called the "Star". The painted stucco work moulded in the form of a vine that it bears upon its facade is quite superb, and, in the Ship's particular setting, highly effective. For the Ship is a tall narrow building placed among mainly uninteresting edifices, but because of its unusual decorative work it is almost impossible to pass it by without wondering what lies within.

What does lie within is a very busy and very efficient City tavern, with bars upstairs and down, in both of which good food is available. The upstairs room is a cocktail bar, while that downstairs has been fairly recently decorated to resemble a ship's cabin, but not in any way ostentatiously.

The Ship is a worthy establishment with which to close this brief selection of City taverns. It lies in a relatively quiet part of the metropolis, a pleasant place to chance upon, only five minutes walk away from the river and close to the Tower of London and Tower Hill, one-time place of executions but now the scene of nothing more violent than sometimes angry speechifying.

The Black Friar
QUEEN VICTORIA STREET

The exterior of this pub is something quite unusual, at the same time pleasant to regard, and it is more than worthy of passing admiration.

It is rewarding finally to cross the Thames, to enter what to many is but a wilderness: "South London". Naturally this is a prejudiced conception; there are pockets of London lying south of the river that are every bit as interesting as those to the north. Southwark, for instance, boasts antiquity that extends back in time fully as far as the City of London itself. Living proof of this assertion is to be found in the presence of THE GEORGE INN, one of the few public houses in London to carry the title "Inn", though strictly speaking it is one no more.

It lies just off Borough High Street (S.E.1.), only two minutes walk away from the southern end of London Bridge, where at one time stood the grisly "Traitors Gate", before which the decapitated heads of felons and traitors used to be set on pikes as a warning to others. The George, as its sign still indicates, used to be called the "George and Dragon". It possesses several unique features that have helped to make it one of the most celebrated taverns in all of London, indeed in the British Isles.

Southwark escaped the Great Fire of 1666, only to suffer one of its own exactly a decade later, and the present building of the George dates from 1677, following rebuilding. The establishment, however, dates from at least as early as 1554, and is conceivably a good deal older. It is a half-timbered structure, with some wonderful old beams in evidence inside and a bar floor that slopes perceptibly with age; it also boasts the distinction of being the only galleried coaching inn still standing in London. Today it is admirably cared for by the National Trust, which now provides the customer not only with a fine physical example of this kind of old inn—where drinks in the bar are still dispensed through a hatch, not as is normal today over a counter—but also with full restaurant facilities, and excellent luncheons and evening meals are to be procured in distinguished surroundings.

The Ship...
HART STREET

Coulstone 73

The George also boasts a courtyard and is completely cut off from the street outside. Originally the inn extended right round this courtyard, but today only one portion of the building is preserved; there is sufficient, for all that, to see how an old coaching inn really looked, and the outside gallery serving the upper quarters still provides the only means of passing from room to room. Traditionally the George's courtyard is associated with the drama, and during Shakespeare's lifetime regular performances used to be given here. It is even averred that Shakespeare himself may have acted in this very courtyard, and since it is pleasant to believe in such a fancy there is no call for disputation. Today, during the summer months on Saturday afternoons, in a natural stage area provided by some old railway buildings, Shakespeare's plays are still given here, and thus the tradition remains unbroken.

Other literary associations may be claimed on the George's behalf. Dr. Johnson may sometimes have come here, for he often visited his friend Thrale the brewer at Streatham, and since Thrale's business lay in South-wark, and the coach to Streatham always called at the George, the two friends could easily have started their journey from here. Similarly Dickens can be linked with the George: in his novel "Little Dorrit" he caused Tip to use the George as an address for writing his begging letters to Clenman, and this surely points to Dickens himself having known the inn well.

"Historic Southwark" is the usual epithet applied to this borough. There are places of interest in profusion here, including the cathedral church of St. Saviour that is famous mainly for its literary associations. As a link with the George Inn which it lies so close to, it may be mentioned that in this church, in 1607, was buried one Edmund Shakespeare, "player", brother of the great playwright and who almost certainly would have acted in the George yard at some time during his career.

For a final tavern to be included in this selection it will be pleasant to turn to an establishment in Rotherhithe Street (S.E.16), overlooking the Thames and lying at some distance east of the George. It bears the name of THE MAYFLOWER, although it originally went under the name of the "Spread Eagle and Crown". The name was altered to mark Rotherhithe's connection with the Mayflower, which just before setting sail on its momentous voyage was moored in the Thames close by.

The George Inn...
SOUTHWARK

Captain Christopher Jones, its commander, came from Rotherhithe, and his remains now lie in St. Mary's Church just adjacent to this old tavern.

Rotherhithe lies in Bermondsey, a part of south London that does not often appeal to the tourist and yet abounds in places of historic interest and boasts a proliferation of good public houses. The Mayflower is perhaps pre-eminent among them in terms of picturesqueness, with a wooden terrace at the rear stretching out over the Thames and providing a wonderful spot for summer evening drinkers. Inside it is easily possible to be transported back a couple of centuries or so in time. The wood panelling and low-beamed ceilings are perfectly genuine. Certainly the Mayflower is a show-place; it is also a most proficient public house which provides excellent bar snacks as well as full restaurant luncheons and dinners.

The Mayflower makes an ideal tavern with which to close this book, a perfect balance, together with the George at Southwark, for some of the fine old taverns that it has been possible to select in the northern reaches of London, such as the Flask in Highgate and the Spaniards on Hampstead Heath. To mention these four establishments in the same sentence is at once to conjure up images of a distant past, one with which it is still happily possible to commune in some faint way through the pleasing agency of these fine old taverns.

The Mayflower...
ROTHERHITHE